GOSPEL EARTH

the
scriptures
from Golgonooza
for Julia Willis
who hears & sees
Jeffrey
2014

GOSPEL EARTH

Jeffery Beam

He who has seen everything empty itself is close to
knowing what everything is filled with
Antonio Porchia

Gospel Earth

SKYSILL PRESS
3 Gervase Gardens
Clifton Village
Nottingham
NG11 8LZ
skysillpress.blogspot.com

A special thank you to the late Sylvester Pollet of Backwoods Broadsides, Bob & Sue Arnold of Longhouse Publishers & Booksellers, Mark Kuniya of Country Valley Press, Robert Walp of Chester Creek Press, & Richard Owens of *Damn the Caesars* for hearing large portions of these gospels & taking them up. Thanks also to the other editors & magazines that published these poems. The late Cid Corman read & commented on some of these poems; my everlasting gratitude for his mindful & generous consideration. Thank you Joe Massey for encouraging me to begin this collection & to Josh Hockensmith & David Need whose own enthusiasms serve to remind me how much can be said with few words. A cadre of other friends also read & responded to this *Gospel*. I thank them for their close reading, criticism & witness: Simon Cutts, Cy Dillon, Ricky Garni, Whit Griffin, Shauna Holiman, Andrew Hughes, Cralan Kelder, Louise Landes-Levi, Janet Lembke, Ann & Jim McGarrell, Thomas Meyer, Ippy Patterson, David Preece, J. P. Seaton, Erica Van Horn, Scott Watson, Phyllis Walsh & Marly Youmans. Of course, *elation & Clare* to Sam Ward who heard in these old man's gnomic Gnostic utterings some relation to a youthful cosmic urge.

Special thanks to Laura Frankstone for her inspired art.

This big book of little poems first shaped on February first in *Faoilleach* — the Wolf Month — on St. Brigid's Day, or to the Pagan Way, *Imbolc* & the Goddess Brighid — a time of poetry, weather prognostication, healing, purifying fires, smithcraft, sacred marriage, animal divination, corn dollies, ewe's milk & lamb's birth — *Imbolc* being Irish for "in the belly". Moved to the second by the Christians, we now divine the weather on Groundhog Day, instead of with the Pagan serpent or badger. *Thig an nathair as an toll/ Là donn Bride — The serpent will come from the hole / On the brown day of Bride.* Brighid — in three aspects — the Physician, the Smith, the Poet (Dame Kind; the Greek Persephone, Demeter, Hecate — born from the Vedic word *brihati* — the divine) — is the daughter of *Daghda*, chief of the *Tuatha dé Danann*, the Israelites' Lost Tribe of Dan, which disappeared into Northern Europe — becoming the Celts. The hag of Gaelic tradition, *Cailleach*, is said to have been seen on *Imbolc* as a gigantic bird, gathering firewood for winter's continuance — unless she sleeps allowing spring to come sooner. Hence, these little sticks and branches kept from her grasp and brought to you by the poet & Skysill Press to shorten winter's foul dominion, hasten spring's promise.

To Thunder
To the Bright Realm

For One World

&
In memory of
Jonathan Williams
& for
Thomas Meyer

whose friendships & jubilancies
constructed my world

A device
that will not bend or burn
that the turtle might pass
unharmed

Flores McGarrell
(Earthquake, Haiti, January 2010)
For the world's broken heart his mending make

Contents

Travels

Mountains

Honey & Cooked Grapes (France)

Supernatural Songs (Ireland)

Green Man

Burchfield

MountSeaEden

Illuminations

WHAT use is prose when what we are speaking of is the poem? I take up pen finding wide silences that do *not* ache to be filled. Spaces between things & thoughts seek me out. Shadows fill my poems. In that *illumination* is the Word. I seek the Beloved — the pearl ribbons He leaves behind. I listen for silent bells. I smell sweet flowers near the intelligent lowly ground. I look in the last place we would think to — in the discarded shattered world. Someone asked Rumi that if he, indeed, really believed in silence, then why did he talk, sing, & dance so much. He replied, "The radiant one inside me never speaks."

POEMS awkward in construction &, I hope, as I write them, awkwardly human, profess a spiritual landscape which inhabits both inner self & outer ground — my "pelican standing guard" or those "crickets singing at eye level . . . me on the ground with their song" — my body one with spirit & absorbed into the world — which for me is not of warring dualities but where the other & the here & now pronounce their inseparableness. The open-endedness is a path. Antonio Porchia says, "A thing, until it is everything, is noise, & once it is everything it is silence."

UNLIKE many of my southern brethren & sisters, I have few "stories" to tell, although I have often found myself drawn to sequences, & even making books of poems, which recount an interior tale rendered from the body, places, & in the living plant & animal world.

THE SMALL POEM continues to fascinate me too, & I am intent on making something new from the examples found in the spiritual literature & folk traditions of the East & West — Japan, India, China, Korea, & Malaysia — *The Dao*, the *I Ching*, canny Biblical fragments, the Desert Hermits, Gnosticism, Sufism, Ancient Greek poets & philosophers, the French & Spanish

I

Surrealists, the Symbolists & Decadents, Shape Note songs, bluegrass & African-American gospel music, women's poetry throughout time, Native American poetry, & the poets of the contemporary small poem movement in America & Britain — particularly Bob Arnold, Thomas A. Clark, Cid Corman, Simon Cutts, Ian Hamilton Finlay, Harry Gilonis, Grant Hackett, Cralan Kelder, John Martone, Joseph Massey, David Preece, Erica Van Horn, & Scott Watson. Always, & always the vatic intensities of Akhmatova, Ammons, Basho, Berryman, Blake, Bly, Broughton, Bunting, Carson, Cavafy, Celan, Char, Chopra, Clare, Claudel, Leonard Cohen, Cummings, Dahlberg, Dante, Dickinson, Donne, Duncan, Eliot, Emerson, Follain, Robert Francis, Frost, Garcia Lorca, Genet, Ghalib, Jack Gilbert, Louise Glück, Goyen, Gregg, H. D., Ignatow, Ikkyu, Issa, Ronald Johnson, Carl Jung, Kabir, Keats, D. H. Lawrence, Laughlin, Doris Lessing, Levertov, Merwin, Thomas Meyer, Henri Michaux, Millay, Joni Mitchell, Moore, Neruda, Niedecker, Mary Oliver, Joel Oppenheimer, Patchen, Plath, Ponge, Antonio Porchia, Rexroth, Rich, Rilke, Rimbaud, Roethke, Jamie Sabines, Sandburg, Santoka, Sappho, Sei Shōnagon, Shakespeare, Edith Sitwell, Stevie Smith, Sri Aurobindo, Stevens, Stein, Thoreau, Thomas, Vallejo, Whitman, Jonathan Williams, William Carlos Williams, James Wright, & Yeats. This is my family tree. Their names, music to me, as their poems.

OVER eighteen years ago, inspired by Asian poetry, but especially by D. H. Lawrence's small poems & a remarkable little poem, "Hands ... Birds" by M. C. Richards, I began experimenting with small & one line poems. Later Stephen Berg's versions of Ikkyu, *Crow With No Mouth*, confirmed the energy of the one-liner & mine began to occasionally coalesce into loose sequences or linked one-liners. I want to invigorate the startling propulsion of haiku's accessible simplicity & minimalism, while creating a more active

2

canvas. I want to contribute to the writing of new Gnostic gospels — inside & out of the Christian & Sufi traditions. The poems frequently root in places I have been & love. I find it humorous, & so like me, to make such a big book ... of little fireflies. May they glimmer large.

Sorrow the Awakener was given to me in 1996 by Dr. J. N. (Jehangir Nasserwanji) Chubb, my Vedic philosophy teacher, during an especially challenging period of my life. He wrote this poem at a similar time in his own life when he was a very young man. Born in 1910, a noted philosopher & teacher of Eastern & Western thought, & a devotee of Sri Aurobindo, Dr. Chubb passed away in 2001 in Auroville, India. This poem continues to be a touchstone, a lodestone, a reminder, a beacon, & prime inspiration for the writing of *Gospel Earth*.

Heal Ourselves. Heal the Earth.

Jeffery Beam

A Gathering of Voices

In it what is in it
                —Jalaluddin Rumi

Truth is One & the learned call it by many names
                —*Rig Veda*

Brag, sweet tenor bull
                —Basil Bunting

You have slept for untold ages, this morning will you not awake?
                —Kabir

O / let us give stems to / the flowers! / / Substance to this / fog
                —Ronald Johnson

If flowers are abundant then they are lilac, if they are not they are white
in the center
                —Gertrude Stein

Despite constrained petals / the bud opens
                —Thomas Meyer

The words the happy say / Are paltry melody / But those the silent feel
/ Are beautiful
                —Emily Dickinson

Earth, my likeness
                —Walt Whitman

Live yourself / straight through, without clock
                —Paul Celan

5

I think of a tree / to make it / last
     —Lorine Niedecker

I sing the grass that is born with me
     —Pablo Neruda

I swallowed the god in my mouth
     —James Broughton

Every blade of grass has its angel that bends over it & whispers, "Grow,
grow"
     —*The Talmud*

To walk in the grasses / to linger in the forest / & feel it to be true
     —Thomas A. Clark

Whatever it all is it is all blossoming
     —Santoka

Music speaks to music — how else could I reach you?
     —Cid Corman

The wise know nothing at all / well maybe one song
     —Ikkyu

More beauties / than I / can find / room to / talk about
     —John Clare (channeled through David Preece)

Outside where / the world's a storm / in the oaks / & the outcry of
certain / beautiful captures
     —Jonathan Williams

That in black ink my love may still shine bright
　　　　　—William Shakespeare

Why the erotic matters so much. Not as / pleasure but a way to get to
something darker. / Hunting down the soul, searching out the iron / of
Heaven
　　　　　—Jack Gilbert

Oh, how sweet was the earth for me with you
　　　　　—Anna Akhmatova

More than most men he could half-inhabit / some old tree, perhaps, or
some new cloud
　　　　　—Robert Francis

Nothing that is not there & the nothing that is
　　　　　—Wallace Stevens

One by one objects are defined — / It quickens: clarity, outline of leaf
/ / But now the stark dignity of entrance — Still, the profound change
/ has come upon them: rooted, they / grip down & begin to awaken
　　　　　—William Carlos Williams

I returned / smiling & haunted / to a dark morning
　　　　　—Denise Levertov

Where you are lying / secret of the world / with so strong an odor?
　　　　　—Jean Follain

You are that vast thing that you see far, far off with great telescopes
　　　　　—Alan Watts

My images stalk the trees & the slant sap's tunnel
　　　　　—Dylan Thomas

God made you thus. / To pleasure us / Against out dying
                    —James Laughlin

For mere incidence into / the hush of meaning
                    —Mary Oliver

We see another world alive / & our wholeness finishing
                    —Linda Gregg

The darkness lifts, imagine in your lifetime ... / & the soul creeps out of
the tree
                    —Louise Glück

There is a crack in everything. That's how the light gets in
                    —Leonard Cohen

If there is a place where this is language may / It be my country
                    —W. S. Merwin

Tell me where is fancy bred
                    —William Shakespeare

The air was watching watching. / The air watched all night long
                    —Federico Garcia Lorca

Yet resurrection is a sense of direction, / resurrection is a bee-line
                    —H. D.

If I were not here; & I am alien; a bodiless eye; this world would never
have existence in human perception
                    —James Agee

I will submerge myself within a celestial earth
                    —René Char

If I find you I must go out deep into your / far resolutions / & if I find
you I must stay here with the separate leaves
    —A. R. Ammons

I had love's body, knew those intoxicating lips
    —C. P. Cavafy

I am circling around God / around the ancient tower
    —Rainer Marie Rilke

From the most sacred waters I returned / remade in the way that trees
are new
    —Dante Alighieri

Do you mean to tell me you will see no tissue? / Do you prefer to look
on the plain side?
    —D. H. Lawrence

Purge the flesh & you canker the spirit
    —Edward Dahlberg

Suddenly I saw at my feet, / Spread on the floor of night, ingots / Of
quivering phosphorescence, / & all about were scattered chips / of pale
cold light that was alive
    —Kenneth Rexroth

There is a joy here / in being able to handle / so many differences
    —David Ignatow

O Transcendent Therapist / recondition me
    —James Broughton

And the eye bleeds fire / & the earth & dried leaves of the garden / are
lit up because of me
    —Ghalib

We suggest that the great surprise that lies ahead for humanity is waking up to oneness & love
—Timothy Freke & Peter Gandy

Great flaming God, bend to my troubles, dear
—John Berryman

Oh God how sorrowful we have made each other ... / how rich / how forced into melancholy / & into shadowed fortresses of hope / hung with lichen, ferns, rocks, broken sunshine's needles / & the moon's wayward envious watch
—César Vallejo

A quiet root may know how to holler
—Anne Carson

Beyond living & dreaming / there is something more important: / waking up
—Antonio Machado

I am not I. / I am this one / walking beside me / whom I do not see
—Juan Ramón Jiménez

The word of Things a picture is
—Simonides

Humanity is the measure of all things — both of the things that are, that they are, & of the things that are not, that they are not
—Protagoras

An Invocation

To all those suffering, involuntarily, from their imaginations

—Henri Michaux

An Invocation

From cedar's green feathers   cedar's red odor
From moss's cool fever   earthworm's glowing
From pitch-pine's field-taking   pitch-pine's black tarring
From the heel-worn path   eye-light roaming

From cornfield's stalking   bobwhite ascending
From the cardinal's scarlet   a royalty before us
From persimmon & apple   urgent oriole feeding
From blue-eyed grass in shadow   late summer's Eden

From footstep to cow path   mud pool & duck quack
From goldenrod's augur   winter gathers
From ice cracking oak limb   frisson & weeping
From beech leaf in winter   gold filigree forming

From rosehip & goldfinch   thorn & bright needle
From storm clouds gathering   light darting through us
From April's spring torrents   creek's roaring persistence
From pond over-flowing   swamp's restraint ending

From the word unblemished   robust declension
From honesty in bloom   articulate blue
From granite to flagstone   columbine freshes
From cat-paw & wind-blow   soft goes the morning

From Star of Parnassus   tourmaline greening
From bluestem   the meadow
From poplar   the tulip
From each handshake taken   a prayer advocated

From beehive   golden coagulate bomb
From bottomland quiet   no petulant view
From squash bloom   a shine
From dog sleep   a rumble

From peril no thunder   only dwellings to calm
From muscadine's favor   copper infusion
From mountain in snow light   a rabbit's furred thicket
From everything under   a thistle be thine

From garnet & hawkweed   the owl & the red-tail
From trout ever jumping   the roe of attention
From pecan & walnut   bread everlasting
From collard & field green   canny pot liqour

From bluet & aster   concealment never
From wild carrot   the umbel of consciousness feeding
From myself & from strangers   the friend ever trenchant
From mystery's bedroom   love's tortuous wisdom

From the formless   the formed
From the void   all-in-all
From the patient rose blooming   the perilous night
From dove coo at morning   to midday's recountal

From magnolia camellia gardenia   thrall
From dancing thunder   a ridgepole at last
From solitude   vibrant fortitude's castle
From abundant forgiveness   compassion's great tact

From whatever you do or not do   find a meadow
From the river crossing   an island encountered
From the spirit descending   a wine glass uplifted
From evening's quickening   harmonious rest

From the secret unfolding   the obvious moment
From whirring cicada   velvet occasion
From apple forbidden   knowledge abounding
From the snake on the path   origin & ending

From sunlight through trumpet vine   flame in the belly
From tears' shivering sorrow   joy reshaping
From veronica & chickweed   earth warmly responding
From mountain's re-greening   eye filled with blue

The Light Begins

After the final no there comes a yes & on that yes the future world depends

—Wallace Stevens

•

As I went to sleep last night after beseeching whatever help I could — I was much distressed — I was hit by something on my forehead — not light, not the feeling of a real fist — but a distinct sensation of force colliding with skin — a sheath of protection dropping over me. It had no emotional content — very plain & simple — as if a door or window had closed, or a curtain been quietly drawn.

The Light Begins

First
           settling dust among
corn rows
                     circling
ravens holding the blue
black funeral cars almost
                     invisible
Behind their wings behind
the trees the hills
pink fires spread
slow contagion

It was like this the first evening
& one day in the future
                     far
which is also now

Snake in the Garden

Under dry maple shadow
creeping cedar painting
shadows greener
hiding split darknesses
under dissected leaves

The ineffable awaits you

Poised to bite

Welcoming you

Revelation of Melancholy

Despair in the elms
Bitter
      orange in the heart

Four pigeons on
                 a limb
One
    flies off
Now
    all gone

Revelation of Beginnings

The cities pray but
not for long
Soon they will bend

Wind
Tall grass

Paradiso

I go where
feathers blow

World

In the Mimosa Tree

Words came to me & oh they smelled peach but shaggy

Night Gospel

Moon bronze cup

Every Knee Must Bow

Blue shade:

trumpet vine obeisance
to honey bee

Blesséd the Poor

Having nothing

This poem
my net

Errant dandelion

To William Carlos Williams

Dr. Williams it's
not enough that your
poems sting with

innocence
gaiety &
passion
Their forbearance in

the face of human
folly & strife
pricks

sweetly like the rose
of which
you so often
wrote

Treatise of the Daisy
For Daisy Thorp

Luxuriant sun blooming
on infertile ground

Day's eye
brighter
for clouds
breaking round it

Dusk:

Fallen moon a thousand
times on grass

The Hummingbirds

Twilight
The male's throat fire
& ruby prowess

The female
subtler

Her light
simpler

Wings:
earthquake
flash
in air

29

Tree Parable

Rarity red
           tints sourwood leaf points

Each cell a Spanish womb a dove
burning to confession

Thrush's Parable

Tree

Sermon

Day lit shriek opening an awl in the sky owl

Testimony

Silence
                    Fullness

Wait!

          Outside

                    whippoorwill knowing
no time

The Book of Nuthatch

With a flick of

        sunflower seed shell
               a cut —
a thrust —
      explaining
            itself to
sun

Mourning Dove

Tame as love
turning on coralline feet
Scratching at mine

First one then another pine
straw's resiliency strength

Castle-in-the-making

Penitent

Offering feathers
to the moon won't do nor lamps
blueing grizzled sky

Night Jar

detonates the woods
A hungry moth beats its face against a flower

World's heartbeat

The Orderly Processions

No hearts with damaged values

Nature's
        intention:

flight
of wings

William Morris'

hand in the weather
Acanthus leaves English oak leaves
Tongues of fire on earth

Ice patterns on glass

Nyssa sylvatica: Black Gum
For Moreton Neal

Black-green leaves
                    masking autumn oxblood to come

Your shoulders'
urgent blushing
                    as the heart beneath
flushes:
          all hues captive

Headgame

Coarse silk rubbing my brow
Furrows & wind tunnels
The door shuts twice

Winter Homage

Black moss a bird's still eye my infinite room

Lovers' Wisdom

Panting in grass beneath high air sun

Sacred Marriage

Swaggering kisses along needled forehead terraces

Baptism

Red ash rains
Your breath:
                   articulate

When light descends give
sorrow a tender
weeping a hair

Stranger in a Strange Land

Bees sense crowshadow across dry pavement

I am pilgrim on this vegetable earth

Crucifix

Robin wrestles worm into witch-hazel air
Suddenly air serene still as mother's milk

Mountain Bluebird

Flint vein darts from roost

Who among us has seen sart mountains
damaged by fog but
                  that bird

Angels blow liquid fire into that heart
to waken its chortle Ellington blue note vibration

Winter is the world, summer the other realm[*]

Dirt dauber's black iridescence drinking from cat water bowl
Does love's pain diminish or heighten this?

[*] *Gospel of Philip*

Fern Gospel

Red ferns curling in dappled wood beyond

God Comes to See Me

God comes to see me
Without Bell

Never comes with Drum
But shakes the Footings

Of my House
With Subtle Water's roar

Listening at Crown of Day
When Nothing has been said

The Water takes my Breath away
The Landscape's recompense

Commentary on *Duende*

I thank you for
this immense
sulfurous melancholy

Despite the sirocco
the miracle happens

Prunus mume Sutra
Cid Corman (1924-2004)

Cold March apricot air sun shines small upon new green leaves
A moth last night porch light's apricot "summertime"
A few snowflakes fall apricot's porcelain pink remains
Word be with me name the apricot wordless
He's gone what new light in their blossoming

Letter to Meteor

As if in this place giants once lived
rocks redden at dawn
                              again at dusk

Evening:
                    strange light
inarticulate

Then
          out of nowhere
a grace
          a valley bottom

Bomb

So the high pasture

       tenders them
tearing their scent
       across the wide hill
sky bending down
       to meet them

What is here
       What bleating bell beneath
mountain's green sun
       What hoof print writing
horns arched
       locked in rhythm

Memoriam
Robert Creeley (1926-2005)

Beyond the old cornfield a train
Fox looks up — busy world

I lift my bucket to the wintry stars
Out falls emptiness & glass

Mind bears all away
Somewhere order disorder
ripe cherries & wine

Which way to nowhere
Spring sun shows the easy way
Right up through the trees

Secret Gospel

The other world lord
with his rain buckets splashing
with his heart coming a wind
with his translucent looks ravishing
with his copper-ring circling his head
with one river rising
with one river emptying

He keeps turning round the certain mountains
Bringing me back
My seaweed skirt shivering emerald
So I can say the unsayable

To live is to sleep
Awakening the first longing
at dream's gate

Earth Gospel

Expressive
             the world's hills
             earth's convincing boundaries
Now sharp horizons
Now gentle plains
Holy groves
             abstract slender

Eye travels up
beyond dipping ridge
to dwarfed valley below
to our fated knowledge
heavy with cicada song
where strangers may pass &
dark hate dissipates forever

Reconcile hill
to valley

Reconcile intervening time

Fall into clarity completeness

Inner Light

I have seen it when I remember to forget to look
when I remember it is there with my back turned my heart
towards it surf bringing up tarnished impossible boats
through brackish waters & countless smooth pure sands

Resurrection

What late fire-dragons
fume from my body
What purples
What frosts

The night tastes bitter

Dawn's
moss on my tongue

Beauty

Helios Gospel

Standing naked in the sun I
am not like a wolf because

I am the sun

Travels

Givenness of the timeless

—Aldous Huxley

MOUNTAINS

Red Read

Is that redbud blink
or cardinal's eye
below the windblown
new moon?

Foggy Mountain Sutra

Black shadows in the room outdoor fog at bay
Fog drops shadow drops transparence window

In limitless fog branches silhouetted against gray dawn
Who are you now

Beyond thick mist sky beyond thick mist sun
Who knows where light sleeps

Close your eyes clock ticking
Open them clock ticking still

Fog night's gray feathers down lifted
Fog dawn's gray feathers at rest

Lift fog from gray-black beech limbs find black-gray fog

•

See me in the green by fog world's ocean
Illusion doesn't want me fog needs me

A fog hat on the fern fronds a frog plop on the frog pond

Marl grass blanket for winter's beetles no birds fly

Halfway up slope spring burbles into fog morning
Not only water not only sound

I hunger for all I don't see
What sees me hungers more
World without foggy end

Anxious to waken anxious to go out
What gray bones dance me to my grave

Mountain pillows to rest fog cushions in dream's land

Why keep dreaming loss fog filters eye iris
Fog thickens blood love stiffens love

Still night lingers fog holds sun in its cup
Waiting for the right moment now

little: a Happy Hill Sutra

For Stanley Finch, Thomas Meyer, Georgette Williams, Jonathan Williams
& for all the Little People in the worlds (ours & theirs),
All of us have not forgotten you

I come to crush time to study you to teach
                    —The Buddha

Little enough said little enough thought little
enough forgotten little enough

Porch's cold concrete bumble bee's raftered
catacomb fog lifting

Bat mother in porch eave tell us your favorite supper

Incessant wren listen cars climbing the mountain
one mouth feeding another

Doves weeping on boughs dawn rain

Gay feather in daylilies splinter in finger

In the dress shop peonies in the garden
peonies in the mind one

My pockets empty wren hopping cricket death
chicks cheeping no rain today

Two green grasshoppers bathroom's red walls
you looking in mirror too

Wasp carrying green worm back again one minute here
one minute gone Sisyphus or Sage

Mournful crow fireflies where are you Gods
& Goddesses fern fronds

Negative space no Positive space on

Fingers aflame with spring water nothing lasts

Not this not that white shadows on the hemlock boughs

Too much said too much thought too much
forgotten too much

One day a man came I am not he observe

HONEY & COOKED GRAPES (France)

For Marda Burton, Stanley Finch, Anna Hayes, Patricia Owens

yellow green in the gray dawn birdsong
one duck searching for summer's worm

Lilac Days in the Lot Valley

Magpies battling on tile roof below the windows
sun setting between steel clouds lilacs blooming

wake up! mind hears bird's green breath responds
wake up! birds hear mind's lilac breath respond

I realize
often unseen
we burst into starry flames
perhaps a nettle
green & less intensely blue
A high entrance
A reassuring yellow
Singing nostalgic romances

& when it is well
add honey or cooked grapes
hunks of bread
& wine then
a full moon rise

Burning spring greens the peasant's breath
night's coming smoke in clouds
smoke in his mossy orchard
not there
but somewhere above him
clouds & breath unite
fading into hidden blue
what he knows fires smoke breath moss
what is unknown welcomes him to its air

Tour de Faure, Lot River Valley

A duck's *ack ack ack*
in the Sunday morning wind
under the gray-blue rain drenched sky
in the lime green light on the morning
mountain in the river valley where
a duck times the wind & the tunnel
made there of light & sound fills
with other birds other whistles & wheeps
other trees the names I have yet to know

row upon row of trees
stitched with mistletoe jewels
green multitudes
Chateau de Luynes

Men of Toulouse

What love to be made with such sunshine in the body

Message

Winds sigh through bare orchards February in Marseille

Green Psalm

walnut tree green emerald leaves golden underside mistral

Black Madonna, Rocamadour

At her back water dripping from cave walls
Diamonds in her crown water rust & diamonds

Minerve

saffron *soufflé* saffron *cremè bruleé* saffron ice cream
walnut tree in mistral Cathare wind
ruins above the plain orange flames
stones broken by sword *consolamentum* saffron incense

RIVER DAYS (Neuse River, New Bern)

For Stanley Finch, Patricia Owens, David Romito, Mary Frances Vogler

Drought

Never mind moonlight liquid on my eye garden
Divine light never ceases

Aurelius says

Let the deity within you be the guardian of a living being
Red on the black gum leaves
Ants crawling on my neck skin tingling
Goldenrod's green gold river wind

Neuse River Poem

long night belly empty mind full pen squeamish for each word
bird flight through lightning wind dark tree
whistle wind whistle rain black snake guarding the garden shed
bird bend low into west-ridden water gray crest gray sunset rain
coral snake slithering across porch where's my flashlight tonight
lightning bolt answer my question
show me my thought splitting black water-rain heartbeat
tonight Zeus tomorrow Thor midnights of the sun
afternoons of the storm

Crab meat tasting of origins
Moonlight tasting of cloud sieve
Dried cherries & wine

Shrimp over fire flame under eyes fireworks over water

Tidal river molten lead sunlit lit
Thin blue clouds gray heron flies

Intelligence deity earth corruption
Cold sun rises over morning river

Dawn's beauty night's beauty
mud going into the rich over into dawn down under

Black snake's old skin rhythm left on porch eye sockets whole
Diamond glitter prime principle

Heraclitus

diamond battalions march across
sun-soaked water in soft wind
onward marching emptiness eager to be filled
emptiness always moving
as the river moves this morning
not the great void not the great
void also longing to be filled
filled with its own bright emptiness
polishing my sadness
fish jumping from
my happy mouth

Dear friend screaming in night terrors
what past life remembers you
This moment your yelp unimpeded by time

Friends cards table hilarity chance
Night falls wine glasses empty
Pelican standing guard
No one wins no one loses

Mother Koan

On her death bed a mother answers her daughter's question
"Do you know who I am?"

Entering the light world mother answers
"Don't you know who you are?"

Humility nourishes everything
Do good so you would soothe
Your face should always be shining

ITALIAN SCENES

For Ann, Jim, & Flores McGarrell

Dear Flores, lost, Haitian earthquake, January 2010

Italian Scene

It is through celebration that we become part of what we perceive; the great arc of birdsong — that runs around the world in the receding darkness & through which we are re-swept into the light of day — is as much part of the dawn as the sun's first flash
         —Norman Mommens

Morning swifts piercing rippled clouds their circling narrows a blue tower
Cypresses between vineyards hillsides hung with goats & stormlight
Villas in rain figs marrying the vine
Perpendicular cliff footpath to cave rosemary midnight crevice
Pick up stone surprise eternal weightlessness how heavy
Straw whispers Goddess's cold breath
Then falling water lemony smoke warm breezes
Pick up stone surprise eternal density how light
We pass a red blaze roasted pears honey wine
Under deepening sky a hundred candles in windows
Simple rapture woman crouching in the garden

Hymn to the South

Pollarded arthritic trees
Olive & thyme clinging in the cliffs' clefts

Swifts, Umbertide

Wisteria's purple hypnotics swifts overwhelming sky
Blue denizens down from octagonal church's battlements

Sins warned away by black night's coming morning

A Little Book of St. Francis

What whispered place from visions spring always springness

Not Afraid

Pale perfect passion disappears
Lizard sunning on stone
Stone sunning on sun

The Visitation: Moth

No flame to explain me

SUPERNATURAL SONGS (Ireland)

This represents irony & this doesn't
This represents war & this does not
This represents something not & this does

Distances

The shortest longest poem:	There
The longest shortest poem:	Here
The longest poem:	Everywhere
The shortest poem:	Everywhere

Walking on Water

Ship heave
blow what you must
from white chant
                rip water
leave behind
                smooth

•

True goddess

delicately sing
watch & blow love light & power
from behind
essentially gorgeous heart

Holy Well

Hot aching bitter dream heaved to wind
Ask Time when the enormous flood will stop ...

Ask away ...
            then sit

The She I Saw in Eire
for Zerifeh Eiley

Jamaican firebird eating an Irish apple morning

Offertory: Blake

for Ippy Patterson

Two moths lay down
Let me find them
Upon a summer's day
All that fenced me in
Forsook me
To give me golden play

Waking the Tree

A sleepwalker
                    springing from seed
Home
        until a bird
emerges:
        flees
                    its unerring roots

Cliffs of Moher

Walking up hill to something other than cliff
Something bigger than majesty's other
No small tranquility uninhabited
Time's endless roaring abyss

Dolmen

Blown back down gyre's guile

Irish Prophets

Rooks rise renounce fading leaf fall
Announce fox lair rockery
Announce blackthorn's winterberry gathering
Clouds shawl Blackstairs Mountains' night

The Vision

Crow black night window beyond sleep beyond dreams wind shifts sky
Tree black full moon silhouette cloud window ceaselessly moving

And Yet

I am alone
understanding the world
shuffles great grievances

& yet

& yet

What is the Sound

of
    before I was born
of
    before I was dead

of
    the broken winged bird

Elegy to the Dead

If we could only control
all the conditions
all the zeroes ones & ...

Green Man

How shall I name you, immortal, mild, proud shadows?
I only know that all we know comes from you,
& that you come from Eden on flying feet.
Is Eden far away, or do you hide
From human thought, as hares & mice & coneys
That run before the reaping-hook & lie
In the last ridge of the barley? Do our woods
& winds & ponds cover more quiet woods,
More shining winds, more star glimmering ponds?
Is Eden out of time & out of space?
& do you gather about us when pale light
Shining on water & fallen among leaves,
& winds blowing from flowers, & whirr of feathers
& the green quiet, have uplifted the heart?

—William Butler Yeats, from *The Shadowy Waters*

Minotaur Exposed

For John Menapace

We shall not cease from exploration
& the end of all our exploring
Will be to arrive where we started
& know the place for the first time
                    —T. S. Eliot

Think often of my eyes:
Through one forged of
steel & glass
I view the world

Eye awakens:
Not the water, but
*a patterned energy made visible**
by it:

Silence
music reaches for:

Still point where
notes gather pattern
path meets pathway

◙

120

If there were a place
I could enter
I would enter it finding
the door in the wall the wall itself

This side that side
vanishes
Endlessly here endlessly not

A door opens:
Neither somewhere nor nowhere
On the other side either
something or nothing

Close your eyes you
hear it

Open them

Is it gone?

I shape wood into mist
I make grasses into water
I grow my hair long
& white

The eye looking straight on hears
the zigzag electric
in the upright thing

There! A crack
in the wall
A moment's verdant skin
dense with ceremony & resemblances

Green will out:

I leave my chambered room
Yet another nautilus summons me
Death's river beyond the courageous door
Living door beyond the tranquil world

Setting forth even lazy boats startle in anticipation

Receive me O compassionate
entrances & exits!

O world made contradictory & real
by time, men, & wander arriving!

I knew you even before my eye
I knew you before the first leap scarred my heart
When love thundered through the corridors
& brutality relinquished me

A Holiness in the wor(l)d
Enter into its courts with praise

* Hugh Kenner

My Birth/day

I came to wildblossopening
in womb's April

The Cook's Song
After M. F. K. Fisher

With the wolf at the door.
Feast. Make the shared chop
the best. Make
the mind miraculously
cunning. Make the toast
butter brown.

Add cream slowly to the roux.
Stir in brandy. The summer
fireworks start, & the heady dish.
Glass in hand
the ominous sky seems very high
above you.

Pleased. Awakened. Herbs.
Sweet butter. Cream.
Long heating in earthenware pots.
We'll drink hot wine,
doze, never regret the new
flavor of the changing world:

a potent saffrony steam —
half kiss — half salute.
For a centerpiece, fresh
avocadoes in a bowl, their
skins waxed. The glass.
Silver candlesticks

handsome in the light.
More zest! That
unexpected taste. Consider
the onion. Consider
the olive. Consider bullfrogs
barking in the pond.

The Listeners
For Jonathan Williams (1929-2008)

ONCE there was a country where bird songs were held in the highest regard. However, as it is with most things humans cherish, they were often taken for granted. Nevertheless, much time was spent categorizing & debating their curlicues' & coo-coos' finer points, preserving much admired songs for subsequent generations.

The preferred method for studying songs involved sitting in a peaceful setting (a garden, a wood, a boat on a pond) & simply waiting for a bird to sing from the branches of nearby trees, the fields' verges, the airwaves of the winds. Many beautiful & unique songs were discovered this way. After many centuries, through such sterling & productive methods of collection, a repertoire became established. The people understood these songs. Even their subtleties were discernible by many, & could be explained to those who could not understand (sometimes in quick order, but frequently in dense & massive tomes).

Unbeknownst to these adoring practitioners of the listening arts, the world filled with thousands of other, perhaps subtler or brasher, unheard songs from birds hiding in bushes or in the deepest woods, on high mountaintops, in noisy city streets, or drifting above the ocean's roar, the earthquake's rumble & the desert's heat. Occasionally, in the evolution of birds, one of these seemingly awkward but equally serious songsters would fly inadvertently by storm or happenstance or curiosity into the domain of the Listeners.

A predictable response occurred: the offending feathered beast would be shooed away at best, & at worst, pelted with stones for disturbing the peaceful poise of anticipated song. Less frequently one of these invaders, perchance by observing & listening, would learn enough sanctioned winning notes & sing. Begrudgingly, almost, these entrepreneurs would be allowed a place on the bandstand.

127

A hundred yeards later, they, too, were part of the canon, often hailed as innovators who changed the way of song forever.

IN this country lived one farmer who since childhood had wondered at the stranger noises he heard on the edge of the fields & woods. Since adulthood, when the crops were in & his other responsibilities laid to rest, he had searched the earth for songs no one had heard.

He was admired for his tenacity, tolerated for his practically querulous obssession with *the other*, smiled at for his foolishness, gently pitied for his ear's loose logic & eccentric tone. Indeed, he had been responsible, at times, for coaxing a rare voice to sing from some tree in a Listener's garden so the Listener could take credit for finding a new but acceptable song.

Most often he was ignored, or at least left to his own too simple or too impulsive devices. *Why he seemed to have no aesthetic, or at least a schizophrenic one!* (Once it was discovered that he could sing with these odd birds, *as if he were one of them*. Most unusual! Most dubious!)

His mind was full of the twittering of birds. His life's work, when not farming, was to preserve the gene pool of song, the primitive, the celestial, & the lovable unloved.

THUS things continued as they always had. While the Listeners held their conferences & wrote their monographs & bibliographies, the farmer wrote furrows in the fields & planted the field within his mind. While the majority preserved the comfortable, though without doubt the oftentimes valuable & beautiful songs, the farmer salvaged & recorded the unknown ones.

It seemed it was meant to be like this & all were happy. The great numbers of unknown, unappreciated, ignored or uncatalogued & secret birds felt a gratefulness that someone, some *one* cared.

128

They could not, however, completely remedy a hint of melancholy in their songs, & truthfully didn't care to. But at other times their potector allowed them to feel the untamed grace of their off-color yet essential notes. Then they would wonder, "Perhaps another world exists, or even many, where a vibrant many-ness holds sway, where one listener's ear, no matter how uncommon its inner workings, is as highly cherished as another's."

AS for you, dear reader, search out a new tree, a different hill, a separate cove. Perhaps a bird of some other song will sing for you, a bird of another color will fly before you, a bird of a variant sweetness, or peep, or trill, or caw, or burp, will fill your ear, gut, or heart today. Who is to say then, for sure, in that other country, whether a bird in the hand is worth two in the bush? We can never know, can we?

Possession Sutra

I knock at
the door

No one answers

I knock at the door
again

No one comes

No one comes
I ask
       Who are you

I am no one
Who are you

Then
No body

The Green Man's Man

The mind, that ocean where each kind
Does straight its own resemblance find;
Yet it creates, transcending these,
Far other worlds, & other seas,
Annihilating all that's made
To a green thought in a green shade.
　　　　　—Andrew Marvell

Green, I want you green.
Green wind. Green branches.
　　　　　—Federico Garcia Lorca

For a long time I
stand at the oak's foot
asking it

what can you tell me of
time　　　　　weather

Its heartbeat doesn't stop
It moves ahead in
its rooted place
swaying its canopy in the wind

Dark wind　　　　　Bright wind
It never says a word
It just keeps talking

◙

131

In order to make sense
of the ground
I build an earthen hill & sit upon it

The ants welcome me as their brother
Bees radiate out in golden circuits
while above the oaks' light-hungry leaves
spread wide   The clouds
call me
                changing their forms

Each day I visit my mound
till one day the rains come

Then I float
happy & wet
among the tadpoles' delight
the moccasins' white-mouthed praise

I ask the wind to carry me
& it does
                Opening my catkins
I make it rain yellow
I make sunshine into powder

I open Nature's book
finding:
The more I know
The less I know

Finding under the oak:
majesty in a creeping snail
deliberation   seriousness
shyness & yet
what absolute trust
the deeply slumbering spirit within *

◧

Once when the hurricane slammed the oak
to the ground
I walked stunned within its branches
elaborate with mistletoe

Girth sacrificed to its friend wind
Dignified even then

◧

Oak:
A garden & country **
Father to perpetual fire
Channel of the gods & goddesses
Opening heaven's crack
Last leaf never falling

I, in my green shirt,
put on my broad antlers
sure-footed, Druidic, lichen-dressed

A wizened-woodman

◙

To entice the eye
into the mysteries of time & weather
I sprout leaves

◙

The oak my father

Twig in winter
Bud in spring
Leaf in summer
Acorn in autumn

◙

All that I am:

A woodpecker at dusk & dawn
on the white oak trunk

A cardinal flower at field's edge reading cloud shadows

The cardinal points — every direction a good & purposeful one

Every oak an axis through earth's center

回

Ah, the lacewing's found the horn-of-plenty at the oak's foot

回

Sometimes I think there are two of me
for my arms are so big I embrace so much
It just doesn't seem that I can be just one

But then One is what I am &
like being
as all oaks are One Oak
as all rivers roar into One

回

I sit at my table counting
the times an acorn hit me
on the head
or the times I looked up straight
up into glinty leaf frissons
when the sun's brevity broke
through the multitude &
I, too, looked down at myself
Green thought in a green shade

◳

The blue jay quarrelsome as
he is

        has style

For this the oak befriended him
Together they made a forest
one

        acorn
        by
        one

* Lorenz Oken in *Textbook of Nature Philosophy,* 1810
** Old English tradition

Notes for *The Green Man's Man* on the occasion of the retirement of Ken Moore as Assistant Director of the North Carolina Botanical Garden

DYLAN THOMAS'S "force that through the green fuse drives the flower" alludes, at least in part, to the primal energy signified by the Green Man. Thomas portrays the force's potent urgency toward deterioration & death, but the Green Man's energy, even then, despite Thomas's depressive assessment, brims with fecundity. A figure of unlimited vegetative force, the Green Man appears in many cultures & in many disguises. He survives as both pagan god & Christian icon. In the greater archetypes he is the dying & reviving god of ancient religions, & the Sacred Tree as depicted in the *Vedas* & in Norse mythology. One can catch a glimpse of him, not yet quite overcome by green, in Neolithic imagery, in Tammuz of the Babylonians, in the Egyptian god Osiris, in the Dionysian Mysteries, & in Cernunnos (*Kur-noo-nohs*) of the Celts. We also sense him in the divinities of Jainism, the American Indian, the Brazilian forest, & in the Aztec god Xipe Tótec (whose "heart is emerald"). He lives in the tales of Robin Hood, Jack-in-the-Green, the King of May, & *Sir Gawain & the Green Knight*.

THE GREEN MAN'S fertile residence within Christian iconography concentrates, as in no other mythology or religion, in the figure's head. In the West, the oldest type manifests as a single leaf or many leaves forming a male head. In another, vegetation disgorges from his mouth, & even sometimes from his ears & eyes — forming his hair, beard, eyebrows, & moustache. Finally, in some, his face materializes as fruit or flower born & nestled within the green. His eyes always look at us from the original spring.

137

FOR ME, the Green Man lives most in the Sufi being, Khidr (a *wali*, or enlightened one, sometimes called a prophet or even angel), known as the Verdant or Green One, whose footsteps leave a green imprint. He appears unexpectedly to the true aspirant & inspired poets when they least expect him & most need him. Khidr, in my opinion, is in all probability the strongest influence on our most familiar church images of the Green Man. After the conquest in the West, Arabic masons & carvers shared not only their highly evolved technical skills, but also their stories, with Romanesque & Gothic artists. Present before then in western culture, the Green Man, at this point, solidifies his power as Christian icon. As a symbol of resurrection & regeneration his image becomes integral, especially from the 11th to the 16th centuries, to many of the great cathedrals & wayside churches of Europe.

THE GREEN MAN is not separate from us; he is our source, emphasizing & celebrating the positive creative laws of Nature, the native intelligence that shepherds & protects this world, & the ecological rightness that guides us. The Green Man reveals & bestows life's mysteries — indeed, he embodies them — generating in us the impulse to personify anything that deeply moves us, & compelling us to plow our hands into the soil where his promise dwells, nestled in Persephone's arms, perpetually ready to germinate in & nurture the world.

Burchfield

Does the ember glow / in the heart of the snow?

—H. D.

Cicada

Terrible night
Storm yet to come
Cicada drum

Entering No Exit

Another field cloudless sky becomes a revolution

Praise Singing

I am the field alone horizon little eye big world

Burchfield

He loved his river the same way
First time this year wren song

Snow Gloom

All the beauty I wish for
Here at my feet
White earth blue sky white smoke
Ice hidden in little turf depressions
Safe from the sun
Leaving the town to watercress & sleeping crickets

I make drawings of grain

Tremendous dignity
Mysterious air
Some strange rite left clear
Watercolor
Grassy bank

Pigeons, &

dull glass
through which to view them

Mating Dance

Eternal summer
electrifies
the fireflies:

the dream rekindling

Transfiguration Hymn

Black tree phantoms full moon silver
Insects over asphalt

Annunciation

Through a summer storm road confused then weeds
House down below beyond raw sunshine the young birch
Sky again green bloom on whorled leaves
In temporary shadow wren song

Summer's Field

Air so laden the body rains
Goldfinch's feasting trill summer's last sullen green

Revelation of the Cloud

wind clouds boom
the hubbub starts again

Bitter Honey

My summer sweet sweat

MountSeaEden

Traversing the Healy Pass, Caha Mountains, Beara Peninsula, Ireland
Autumn 2006 — traveling companions Stanley Finch, Patricia Owens

Recalling, too, my Appalachians, Autumn 2007

I prefer the streams of the mountains to the sea

—Simon Cutts (channeling an anonymous traditional Cuban song)

Where does today begin in the hills / When yesterday has not fell off?

—Muriel Earley Sheppard

The sea is circled & sways / peacefully upon its plantlike stem

—William Carlos Williams

Beyond all things is the ocean

—Seneca

For a mountain is something high & blue within oneself

—V. S. Pritchett

Now I hear the sea sounds about me

—Rachel Carson

In the awakened eye / mountains & rivers / completely disappear

—Musö Soseki

I once
        took the sea

                        to the mountains

I would rather
        take the mountain

                        to the sea

.

Birds
      white ones
with black wings
above the boat

Above the mountain
they were
           a different
blue

Looking up mountain horizon

I saw it looking down

Sea horizons

                      never stop

Never stop

               Beyond me to

        I Am

In the sea

        order flows

On the mountain

        flows order

Mount

Sea

Eden

In the sea

        I saw a mountain

A whale story

Did you

          ever

               float

I did

       Enough said

Forget the sea:

        sea remembers you

Forget the mountain:

        mountain erodes

I climbed a mountain

blue & high
within me

I heard a sea

green-black
within me too

Together:
                    sky

Capricious mountain

                    Capricious sea

No!
     Only me
                longing

Then longing again

Some songs sang
beyond the horizon

A bird in either ether still songs

Sing a mountain:

       banjo & fiddle

Sing a sea:

       dolphin whine
       crab-fiddle

Sea water:

a prism's ripple

Spring water:

drinking scythe

Sea

    ceaselessly turning wheel

    where day paths coral
    where night paths anemone

Sudden ominous shadows

Grey dawn light
                            over the swells
                            over the hills

Spectral birds
Yellowing coronas

Eels in blue haze

Inlets   Valleys
Currents   Streams
Droplets   Leaflets

Tendrils tending

toward algae bloom
toward mossy banks

Sand in sandal

Leaf-print on pillow

O

Green reservoir

O

Blue waterfall

Regarding orders angelic

                    some prefer sea
                    some mountains

Clouds!

The clouds!

Thrifty mountains

        bright & mineral

where herds graze
where saxifrage assumes

Balsam topping mount

Balm

Heath quilting lane

Home

Past fox den
past king snake shining throat windcurrents stream
where mount harbors sea:

Light-filled
aster field

Come morning

        let's

catch sea-foam in a bottle
carry it to the mountain

Listen

I am in the blood of your heart
The breath of your lung
Why do you run for cover
You are from the dirt of the earth
& the kiss of my mouth
I have always been your lover
Here I am

—Emmylou Harris

The Challenge

Shall I tell the tale from the beginning
Love's human face tendered by ache
Timbers falling
Great grief took me felled me
Shall I tell of Dark Dionysius

Shall I tell the tale over waters
Unfathomable waters not telling
Celestial bowl vessel oceanic
Eros rising masculine movement
Great grief took me felled me
Shall I tell of Dark Dionysius

On one side he who acts
On the other that which undergoes
On one side that never telling
On the other that which tells & never is
Great grief took me felled me
Shall I tell of Dark Dionysius

A buck stomps at wood's edge
Trebling light-hearted wind
Snorting clouds in cool fog's morning
Ferns exhilarating their spoor
Great grief took me felled me
I tell of Dark Dionysius

Mystic Eye

Aye I Eye Yeah!!!

Short Wave

yes an of
I es an of
I no an is
I no an is

Long Wave

am me do
am is do
me as
me do

I am Convinced
After Rilke

I have hit upon
a compromise with my great longing
I am convinced
patience is always good
Nothing that in the deepest sense is justified
in happening
                    can remain
unhappened
But now no poetry in me
Only paraphrase

What   *will I do*
Where   *will I go*
Whose name   *will I say*
What breath   *will I feel*

I have hit   Patience

I am   Convinced

Sophia's Fall

Gods tremor in bodiless beards
Goddesses sun into us
against whom their lights now waver

Genesis

Sky
                    a little unearthly help

White ceiling

Separation of Waters

Waterfall favorite tint corners receding

Genesis: Seventh Day

Cool very clear clammy still but sun-quiet vacancies surrounding

Ecstasy's Rib

Some fell shadow some soul forgot

Adam's Gospel

Torso trunk tree

Eden's Tattoo

Fearless confident confidences
A few inches of skin

Life story perfect home

Sweat

Odor first mystified by sun

Cain's Dream

Recalling moments knifed
by sleep

Striking Metal

Cold godfist
dug from soil
when troubles come
I want also
to be shiny

Clean

Grief

A force more legible
than Wheat — more Chemical
than Sun
                    Burning
to the Retina —
a Solubility

The Anointing

I would scream yet my tongue a rose in cool milk

At Delphi

Robin a city bird rarely seen
The blue jay seldom appears
Indigo flumescence may call at morning

A bird may call at morning
Always a different bird answers
Then symphony intensifying then
beautiful dream after all

Noah

Yes, my friend
rain will tell
Blue moon
Sun

Sun

Invite the sun:
Red morning's garment
Bird restorer

To survive
              The sun's pass
              The lightning's strike
              The deluge
              Sulfur rain bitumen rain

When I got home
Self-song
Transparency   Form
Compassionate wings

Indian Summer

Through the body walks a messenger
her ivory hair black with birds
their great wings washing
across the favorite fresh night

Orpheus

I told the birds
My song's a
pyre fit for love

Only the phoenix believed me

What is hidden from you I will reveal to you[*]

All love all light all right

[*] *Gospel of Mary Magdalene*

Answer the Question

Question the answer
Narrow the way this way that way

Bend in the Road

No matter how I played on the peripheries the word was

Problem of Evil

Pain
no longer exists
Rain
no longer falls
(In) different seed

Incoherence: The Crowd

After Valéry

Dazzled by half
Mingling with the vague
Tumult city
Parliaments streets vanishing

I see my way

The Delphic Oracle Speaks

Green being anxious with question
forsake striving for hunger
as bee freedom for solace
as tree sunlit resilience
mewling calf its mother

Waking at night
Orpheus open your scattered eyes
See with multifaceted insect brilliance
the bedpost the window-dark tree
across swooning sky

Beautiful dream after all

Revisiting Eden

Luscious summer visions fall beneath languid

Moon

In the childhood forest

beetles in creekside mud
peering into their black holes seeing everything

What I came here to learn

Summary of Knowledge

Fiddle not
above eternity

*The last shall be first, the first last**
*Many of the first will be last & become a single one****

Perspective closing
Time arrested to the beyond

* *Gospel of Matthew, Gospel of Mark, Gospel of Luke*
** *Gospel of Thomas*

The World of What

What took you to the station
What were you thinking
What did you inherit
What peculiarities did you acknowledge
What should you did you name it
What is cleverness
What urgency became you

Bridge of a Thousand Whys

He worships still elaborate symphony
A thousand woulds world

The Longing: Lost Magnificence Found
After Doris Lessing

Crushing anguish terrible longing
Something out of memory sobbing into exile

One yellow leaf fall
One gold finch startled

I have entered
                    am still within
a room with many doors
landscape before rising sun
quiet flat truthful light

Remove grief:
Put hand in hand

Quiet Storm

In the bunting's blued eye

the enemy
                    the friend

the kiss without within

Pause

before you turn the page

Pause with me ...

There
That's it
The ancient place
The now place

Now go ...

Told in a Dream

My job one raindrop Listen

Sorrow the Awakener
By J. N. Chubb

It is the hand of Love that strikes the blow
For if the dreamer will not break his dream
But in the magic of the twilight glow
Pursues the shadows of the things that seem
Then comes great Sorrow with her rude caress
& shakes the sleeper into wakefulness.
Not always do we wake. So long we've played
With dreams & in their mists our sorrows steeped
That when the quickening hand on us is laid
We deem our visions into life have leaped.
We stretch, not break, our dreams, so backward creep
Into this death in life, this cave of sleep.

ACKNOWLEDGEMENTS

Thank you to the editors who published these poems previously, sometimes with different titles &/or in slightly different form: "Holy Well" "Short Wave" "Long Wave" "Mystic Eye" "Sophia's Fall" "Genesis: Seventh Day" "Bridge of a Thousand Whys" "Elegy to the Dead" "True goddess" "In the childhood forest" "This represents" "A Little Book of Saint Francis" "Distances" – Alpha Beat Press's chaplet *Jeffery Beam's Allnatural Heatsensitive Ganeshaapproved Zuppapoetica Alphabeat Spiritbody Soup*; "The Green Man's Man" – *Arabesques Review*, the North Carolina Poet Laureate's *Poet of the Week* website feature, as a self-published broadside *Green Finch Keening* no. 66, & as an *Empty Hands Broadside* (Country Valley Press); poems in "Honey & Cooked Grapes" (except for "Men of Toulouse" "Green Psalm" & "Black Madonna, Rocamadour") – *Backwoods Broadsides* chaplet; "To William Carlos Williams" "William Morris'" "Bitter Honey" – *blink*; "MountSeaEden" appeared as a limited edition book from Chester Creek Press; "Memoriam" (under the title "Memoriam: Robert Creeley") – *Conjunctions Web Forum*; "Minotaur Exposed" & "Genesis Told" (containing the poems "Sky, a little" "Separation of Waters" "Genesis: Seventh Day" "Adam's Gospel" "Sweat" "Ecstasy's Rib" "Eden's Tattoo" "Cain's Dream" "Revisiting Eden") – *Damn the Caesars*; "Distances" – *Fourth International Anthology on Paradoxism*; "Swifts: Umbertide" "Message" "Hymn to the South" "Italian Scene" – *Frame*; "Possession Sutra" *Gay City* Volume 2; Parts 1 & 3 of "Treatise of the Daisy" appeared previously as part of a self-published broadside, *Green Finch Keening* no. 59; "At Delphi" "And Yet" "Grief" "Noah" "Mating Dance" "Offertory: Blake" (under the title "For Ippy") "Pigeons, &" "The Anointing" "A Day's Eye for Daisy" (Pt. 2 of "Treatise of the Daisy") "The Light Begins" "Not Afraid" *Prunus mume* Sutra" "Testimony" "Waking the Tree" "Walking on Water" "What is the Sound" "Red Read" – *Hummingbird*; "Visitation: Moth" – *Inch*;

"Winter Homage" "In the childhood forest" "Tour de Faure" "Neuse River Poem" "Friends cards" "Italian Scene" "Aurelius says" "Drought" "Genesis: Seventh Day" "Humility nourishes" – in *Musings for Late Autumn* "Poems Small & Not So Small" a small anthology of my poems on The Jargon Society website; "The Vision" "Pause" *My Laureate's Lasso* (North Carolina Poet Laureate Kay Byer's blog for Friday June 12, 2009) *Poet of the Week* feature, "The Cook's Song" – *Knockout*; "Treatise of the Daisy (Part three)" – *Lilliput Review*; "Mystic Eye" "Distances" – Modern Museum's META Museum Project *A Paean to the Puny* catalog for the First International Think Dinky Invitational; "An Invocation" – North Carolina Poet Laureate's *Poet of the Week* website feature, as a self-published broadside *Green Finch Keening* no. 61 commissioned by the North Carolina Writers Conference to honor North Carolina historian William S. Powell, & as a limited edition chapbook in Japanese wraps (Country Valley Press); "Snake in the Garden" "Revelation of Beginnings" "*Paradiso*" "Every Knee Must Bow" "Tree Parable" "William Morris'" "Winter Homage" "Lovers' Wisdom" "Fern Gospel" "Winter is the world" "Helios Gospel" "*Prunus mume* Sutra" – *Origin*; "The Listeners" – *Oyster Boy Review*, & as a self-published broadside *Green Finch Keening* no. 65 for the 75th birthday of Jonathan Williams; "Bridge of a Thousand Whys" – *Poetry Salzburg Review*; "Entering No Exit" "Told in a Dream" appeared sans title – *Roadrunner Haiku Journal*; "Red Read" "Cicada" "Revelation of the Cloud" – *The Solitary Plover: Newsletter of the Friends of Lorine Niedecker*; "Penitent" & parts of the Creeley poem in a significantly different context – *South by Southeast: Haiku & Haiku Arts*; "Sand in sandal" "Tendrils tending" from "MountSeaEden" – *Teeny Tiny*; "Indian Summer" – *The Sun*; "Annunciation" "Praise Singing" – *Tight*; "Answer the Question" "The World of What" – *Versal*; "Minotaur Exposed" *With Hidden Noise: Photographs by John Menapace* (catalog of an exhibition) & in the expanded book version of the same title;

"little" – *What We Have Lost: New & Selected Poems 1977-2001*, as a limited edition chapbook (diminishing books/Green Finch Press), & a self-published broadside *Green Finch Keening* no. 36; "Thrush's Parable" "The Orderly Processions" "Snake in the Garden" "Night Jar" "Winter Homage" "Crucifix" "Winter is the World" "Mountain Bluebird" "Sermon" "Helios Gospel" – *Gospel Earth* (Longhouse Publishers & Booksellers); "Stranger in a Strange Land" "Bléssed the Poor" *"Paradiso"* "Revelation of Beginnings" "Treatise of the Daisy" "Every Knee Must Bow" "Tree Parable" "In the Mimosa Tree" "William Morris'" "Lovers' Wisdom" "Testimony" "Fern Gospel" *"Prunus mume* Sutra" – *Gospel Earth II* (Longhouse Publishers & Booksellers); "The Light Begins" section is also available online at Bob Arnold's Longhouse Publications website as *Gospel Earth*; Two groups of poems were displayed in my photography exhibitions at Through This Lens Gallery in Durham, North Carolina: "Italian Scene" "yellow green" "Lilac Days in the Lot Valley" "I realize" "Tour de Faure, Lot River Valley" "Swifts: Umbertide" "Earth Gospel" & "Offertory: Blake" (*Daedulus Landed Here: Poetic Views – Earthly Travels*, October 20 – November 14, 2006), "Cicada" "Drought" "Foggy Mountain Sutra" "Heraclitus" "The Longing" *"Paradiso"* "Praise Singing" "Told in a Dream" "Winter Homage" "The World of What" (*Not What it Seems*, April 24 – June 19 2010). [Thank you Roylee "Duvie" Duvall — my best friend in junior high, high school & college — for reappearing in my life & encouraging a new use for my eye & ear].

"Sorrow the Awakener" © 2006 Indian Council of Philosophical Research. Published in *Philosophical Papers of J. N. Chubb*, edited by Harsiddh M. Joshi

"Here I am" © 2004 Emmylou Harris

ALSO BY JEFFERY BEAM

The Golden Legend (Floating Island Publications)

Two Preludes for the Beautiful (Universal)

Midwinter Fires (French Broad Press)

The Fountain (NC Wesleyan College Press)

Submergences (Off the Cuff Books)

Light & Shadow: The Photographs of Claire Yaffa (Aperture)

little (diminishing books/Green Finch Press)

Visions of Dame Kind (The Jargon Society)

An Elizabethan Bestiary: Retold (Horse & Buggy Press)

What We Have Lost: New & Selected Poems 1977-2001
(Green Finch Press)
[A spoken word/multimedia 2 CD collection]

Life of the Bee
(Rock Valley Music)
[Libretto for a song cycle by Lee Hoiby]

New Growth — Shauna Holiman & Friends:
New Songs & Spoken Poems
(Albany Records)
[A CD collection including *Life of the Bee*]

Old Sunflower, You Bowed to No One: Poet Lorine Niedecker
[Special supplement to *Oyster Boy Review*]

Gospel Earth & *Gospel Earth II*
(Longhouse Publishers & Booksellers)
[Two chaplet selections and an online chapbook]

On Hounded Ground: Home & the Creative Life
(Bookgirl Press, Japan)

The Beautiful Tendons: Uncollected Queer Poems 1969-2007
(White Crane Books)
[Revised/expanded edition forthcoming
from Circumstantial Publications]

A Hornet's Nest
(The Jargon Society/Green Finch Press)
[compiler/editor — a Jonathan Williams quote book]

Heaven's Birds: Lament & Song
[Libretto for a cantata by Steven Serpa]

An Invocation
(Country Valley Press)
[Limited edition chapbook]

MountSeaEden
(Chester Creek Press)
[Letterpress limited edition]

The Lord of Orchards: Jonathan Williams at 80
[Forthcoming — co-edited with Richard Owens]

Blue Darter — *Jonathan Williams:*
A Bibliography of the Publications & Ephemera 1950-2008
[Forthcoming]

Photo © 2009 Ted Pope

Jeffery Beam was born in 1953 and raised in Kannapolis, a feudal textile town in North Carolina. Beam is poetry editor of the print & online journal *Oyster Boy Review*, & a botanical librarian at UNC-Chapel Hill. His award-winning works of poetry include *The Beautiful Tendons: Uncollected Queer Poems 1969-2007* (White Crane Books [2008 o/p] — Circumstantial Publications [forthcoming]), *Visions of Dame Kind* (Jargon Society, 1995), *An Elizabethan Bestiary: Retold* (Horse & Buggy, 1999), *The Fountain* (NC Wesleyan College Press, 1992), & the online feature *The Lord of Orchards: Jonathan Williams at 80* (*Jacket*, co-edited with Richard Owens, 2009). His new & selected spoken word CD collection, *What We Have Lost*, was a 2003 Audio Publishers Association Award finalist. His art song collaboration "The Life of the Bee", with composer Lee Hoiby, continues to be performed on the national & international stage. The songs & a recitation of the texts can be heard on Albany Record's *New Growth*. A cantata, *Heaven's Birds: Lament & Song*, by composer Steven Serpa & based on three poems in *The Beautiful Tendons*, premiered in Boston in 2008 for World AIDS Day. Among his current projects is the libretto for an opera based on the Persephone myth, children's books, *Blue Darter* — *Jonathan Williams: A Bibliography of the Publications & Ephemera 1950-2008*, a book version of *The Lord of Orchards*, *They Say: a Commonplace Book on Poetry & the Spirit*, another recently completed manuscript *The Broken Flower*, & a work-in-progress *The Life of the Bee*. Beam lives in Hillsborough, North Carolina with his partner of 30 years, Stanley Finch. You can read & hear more of his poetry at his website: www.unc.edu/~jeffbeam/index.html.

Breinigsville, PA USA
14 June 2010

239819BV00002B/2/P